Where is Jesus Hidden?

Maura Roan McKeegan

Illustrated by Lindsay Carpenter

EMMAUS
ROAD
PUBLISHING

EMMAUS
ROAD
PUBLISHING

1468 Parkview Circle
Steubenville, Ohio 43952

Library of Congress Control Num¹. ₃44308
978-1-64585-064-9 paperback | 978-₂ ₃5-065-6 ebook

Cover design and layout by Patty Borgman

For Shaun, Grace, Finn, Declan, and Donovan
—M. R. M.

For my husband and our girls: Maeve, Haydn, Josephine, and Elouise
—L.C.

Jesus has a face like yours,
With eyes and nose and ears—
But sometimes we can't see Him
Even though He's very near.

Sometimes He is hidden,
Or He's wearing a disguise,
But we can learn to find Him
If our hearts will help our eyes.

Can you find the hidden Jesus
In the pictures in this book?
The words in blue will help you
If you're wondering where to look.

Each picture has a Bible verse;
Each verse contains a clue.
Though He might look very different,
He is never far from you.

Where is Jesus hidden?

Jesus' friends said to each other, "Did not our hearts burn within us while he talked to us on the road, while he opened to us the scriptures?" LUKE 24:32

Jesus is hidden in the words of the Bible.

Where is Jesus hidden?

The angel said to Mary, "The Holy Spirit will come upon you, and the power of the Most High will overshadow you; therefore the child to be born will be called holy, the Son of God." LUKE 1:35

Jesus is hidden in Mary's womb.

Where is Jesus hidden?

"An angel of the Lord appeared to Joseph in a dream and said, 'Rise, take the child and his mother, and flee to Egypt, and remain there till I tell you' . . . And he rose and took the child and his mother by night, and departed to Egypt." MATTHEW 2:13-14

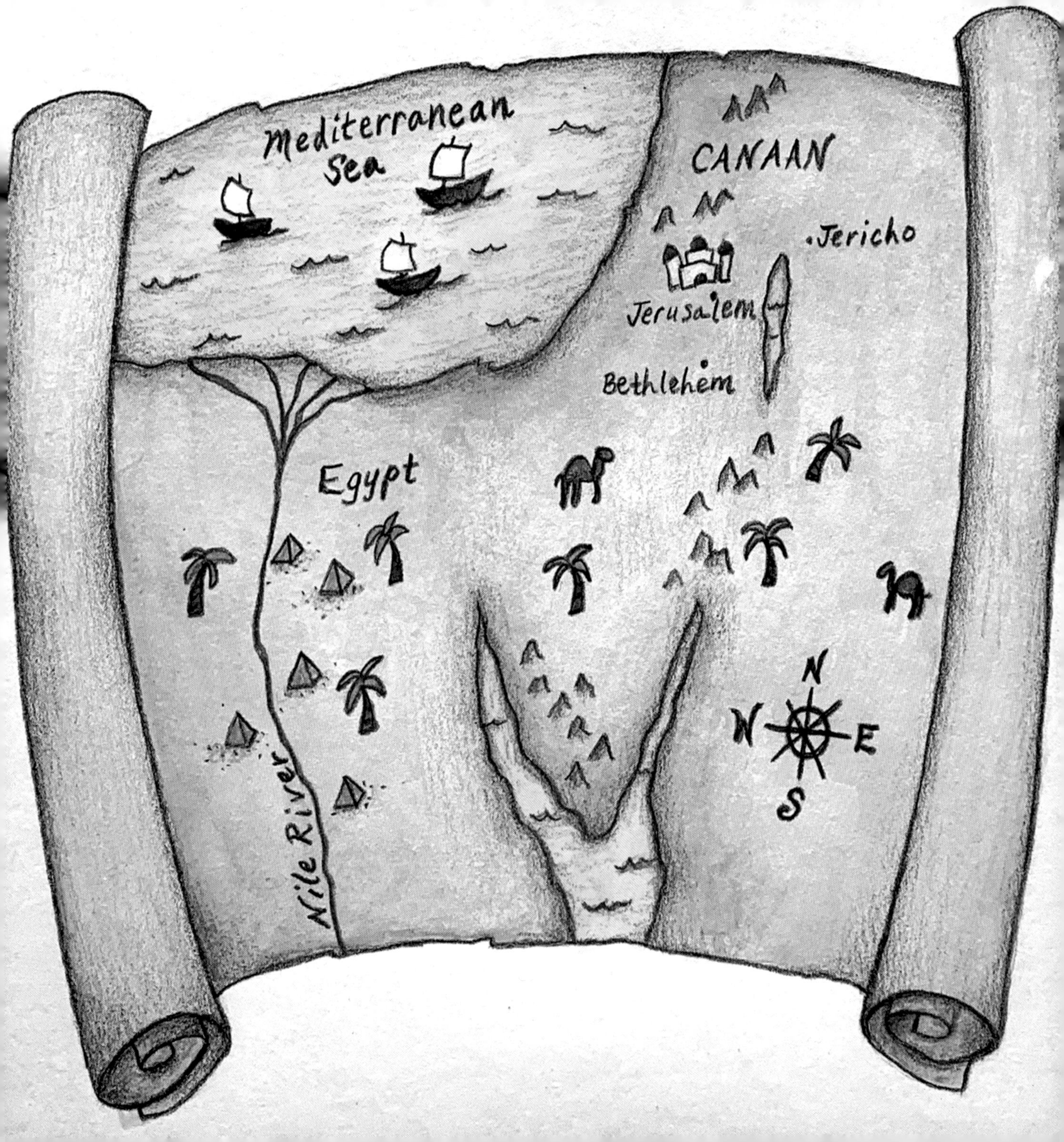
Mediterranean Sea
CANAAN
Jericho
Jerusalem
Bethlehem
Egypt
Nile River
N
W
E
S

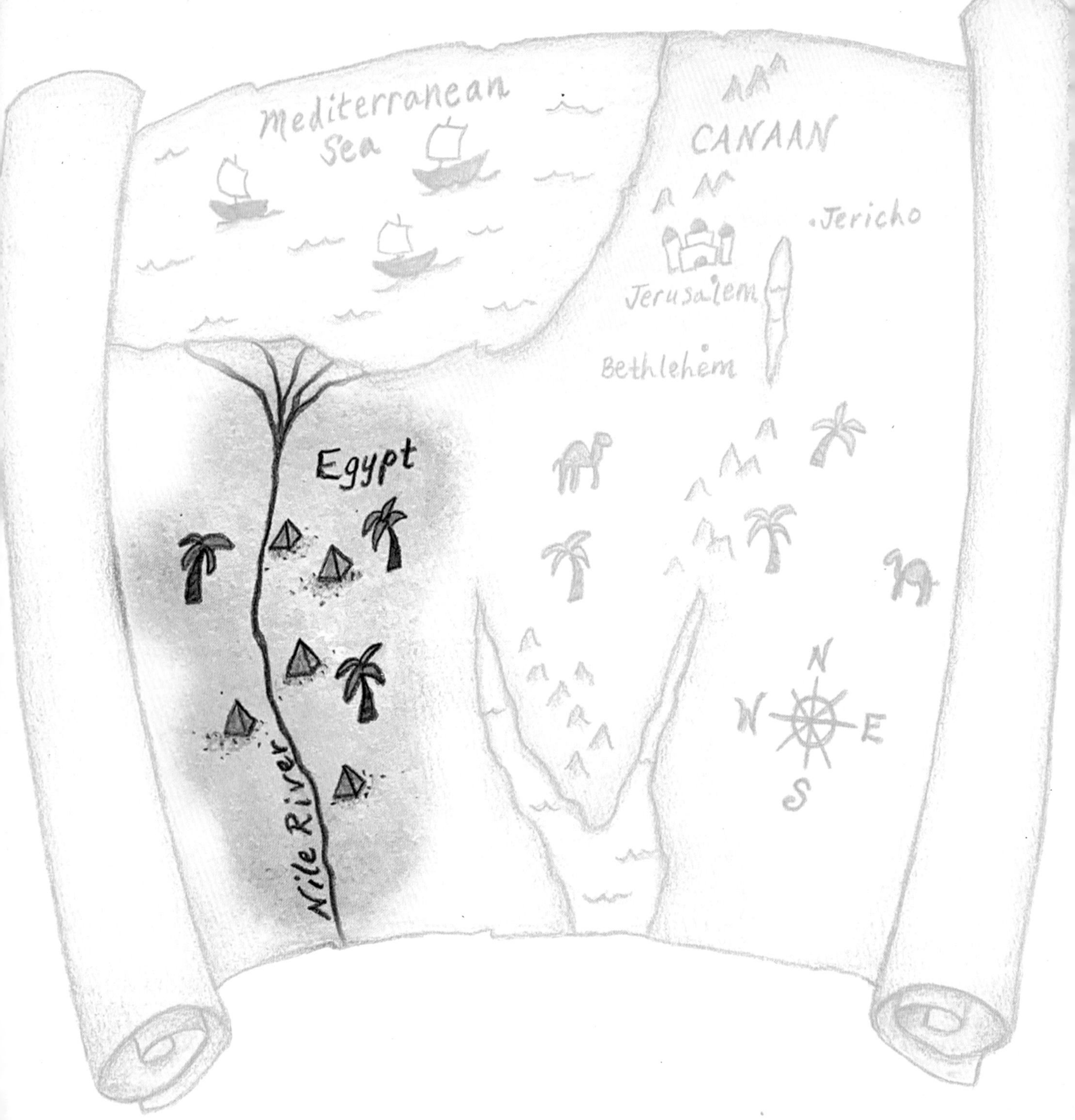
Mediterranean
Sea
CANAAN
Jericho
Jerusalem
Bethlehem
Egypt
Nile River
N
W
E
S

Jesus is hidden in Egypt, where he is safe from King Herod.

Where is Jesus hidden?

"Now in the place where he was crucified there was a garden, and in the garden a new tomb where no one had ever been laid. So ... as the tomb was close at hand, they laid Jesus there." JOHN 19:41–42

Jesus is hidden in the tomb before He rises from the dead.

Where is Jesus hidden?

Jesus said, "This is the bread which comes down from heaven, that a man may eat of it and not die. I am the living bread which came down from heaven; if any one eats of this bread, he will live for ever; and the bread which I shall give for the life of the world is my flesh." JOHN 6:50–51

Jesus is hidden in the Eucharist.

Where is Jesus hidden?

Jesus said, "Foxes have holes, and birds of the air have nests; but the Son of man has nowhere to lay his head." MATTHEW 8:20

Jesus is hidden in people who are poor and hungry.

Where is Jesus hidden?

God said, "Let them make me a sanctuary, that I may dwell in their midst. According to all that I show you concerning the pattern of the tabernacle, . . . you shall make it."

EXODUS 25:8-9

Jesus is hidden in the tabernacle, where the Eucharist is kept.

Where is Jesus hidden?

Jesus breathed on his disciples and said to them, "Receive the Holy Spirit. If you forgive the sins of any, they are forgiven."

JOHN 20:22–23

Jesus is hidden in the priest who hears confessions.

Where is Jesus hidden?

Jesus said, "I was sick and you visited me
... Truly, I say to you, as you did it to one of
the least of these my brethren, you did it to
me." MATTHEW 25:36, 40

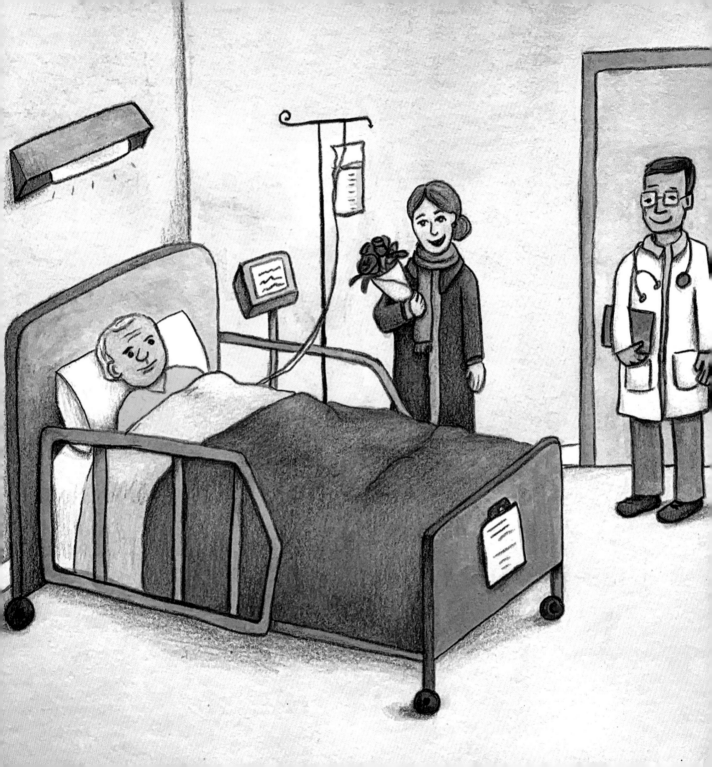

Jesus is hidden in people who are sick.

Where is Jesus hidden?

Jesus "took a child, and put him in the midst of them; and taking him in his arms, he said to them, 'Whoever receives one such child in my name receives me.'"

MARK 9:36–37

Jesus is hidden in the heart of a child.

You have seen the hidden Jesus,
And you've learned where He is found.
Do you know that He is near you?
That He's hidden all around?

Follow where He goes, dear child;
Seek out where He stays.
Search for where He's hiding,
And you'll meet Him every day.